Become the Go to Expert

How to Quickly Create Your Expert Book to Become the High Earning, Go to Expert in Your Industry

Peter Bennett

Published by Peter Bennett
2015

Copyright © 2015 by Peter Bennett

All rights reserved. This book or any portion thereof may not be reproduced or used in any manner whatsoever without the express written permission of the publisher except for the use of brief quotations in a book review or scholarly journal.

First Printing: 2015
ISBN: 978-1-326-36017-7

Peter Bennett
8 Duke Street
Penrith
Cumbria CA11 7LY

www.writemyexpertbook.com

1) Table of Contents

- 2) Introducing Peter Bennett...5
- 3) My Road to Self-Publishing..6
- 4) A Brief History of Self-Publishing.......................................8
- 5) Self-Publishing - An Overview...9
- 6) The Self-Publishing Process..17
- 7) Why Did I Set Up Write My Expert Book?.....................21
- 8) Why Would You Want To Publish Your Own Expert Book?..............22
- 9) How Would That Impact On Your Business?...................27
- 10) Who Would Benefit From Writing Their Own Expert Book'?...........28
- 11) What Could You Call Your Expert Book'?.......................29
- 12) How to Use Your Expert Book......................................33
- 13) Why Become The Expert?..38
- 14) How Is Our Approach Different and Better Than Anyone Else In the Self-Publishing Industry?.......................38
- 15) How Do We Help You Become The Expert?................39
- 16) How can 'Write My Expert Book' help?........................40
- 17) Your Next Step..40
- 18) The future for 'Write My Expert Book'.........................41
- 19) Acknowledgments..41
- 20) References...42
- 21) Resources..43
- 22) Contact details...44
- 23) Special offer...45

2) Introducing Peter Bennett

I was born in London. My father was a curate in Harlington, near Heathrow and I was raised in Zambia and Wrexham, North Wales. Because I was very interested in the science behind everything, I studied for a degree in Molecular Biology at Edinburgh University. I then went on to do three years' post-graduate research in Virology, in London, and then worked in the pharmaceutical industry, running clinical trials. It was at that stage that I sought the help of a Chiropractor for a clicky jaw, and while I was there, she not only sorted out my clicky jaw, but my headaches, nervousness, stomach problems, and all sorts of other things. I ditched the nice job with the company car and started the four year training to become a Chiropractor. My wife wasn't too happy because we'd just had our first child, but I have now been working as a Chiropractor for 15 years and I have never regretted a moment of it; we now have seven children, ranging in age from 20 to 10.

3) My Road to Self-Publishing

Explaining how the science of chiropractic works, and what a chiropractor does, is quite complicated and for that reason difficult to get across. Most people don't really have any idea of what chiropractic is about and most of the time, an initial conversation was spent trying to convince the person that yes, I did know what I was doing, and yes, I could help them; yes, perhaps a physiotherapist would be cheaper and yes, you could just take pain killers. Or I would tell them that they needed to start off with three visits a week, and they would tell me that one visit would be sufficient, and they would drop out as soon as the pain was gone – which isn't the point of chiropractic.

There were many complex issues which made it difficult to run the business, and so I sat down and wrote a book about chiropractic, (which is now available on Amazon), which produced a fascinating result. Not only did the book change the way people saw me, but the referral rate doubled! Before the book patients were very enthusiastic about what we'd done and the results we'd got, but couldn't explain to their friends and family how it all worked because it is so complex. Now, instead of spending hours trying to explain, they can just hand out the book.

Whether they'd read the book or not, people were so impressed by the fact that I had written a book which, in their eyes, made me an expert in chiropractic, that the conversations changed from 'prove to me that I need your services' to 'I'm very interested in your services, do I qualify?'

This complete switch-around in people's attitude made life much easier because people were following our recommendations and, because they were doing that, they were getting better results.

Over the two years that we've been handing out this book, our turnover has doubled and we've gone from being just me and my receptionist, to a practice with two other chiropractors, three receptionists, and a practice manager. The book has made a huge difference to the practice.

It was well worth the time and effort to write my chiropractic book – but it took about nine months of working most evenings and weekends to get it done. Many of my colleagues and chiropractic clients have expressed the wish to write their own book, none of them has been able to spend the time needed to get it done.

4) A Brief History of Self-Publishing

Self-publishing has been in existence since printing began centuries ago, but has only really been available in this particular format for the last 10 years. Before self-publishing companies set up on the internet, there were two ways of getting your book published.

The first was the traditional publishing route, where you got an agent and you approached a big publishing company, who would only be interested if they could sell millions of copies of your book. This was feasible for really big names in a particular industry, such as Tony Robinson, the self-help guru.

The second was vanity publishing where you would pay somebody to get your book published, but then your 2000 copies would sit in your garage, not going anywhere or being useful.

Thanks to the internet we now have the opportunity to easily self-publish a book, and to print very short runs of it. For example, with the chiropractic book, we only publish 30 copies at a time. This helps with cash flow, and if we need more, we just print off more. It's very flexible.

5) Self-Publishing - An Overview

A singer wants to be heard, and a writer wants to be read. Writers are blessed with a unique talent with words, which they have to spread in the world. If you got inspiration to become a writer from an excellent piece of writing work by your favourite author, then it is the right time to consider self-publishing and traditional publishing. Terms may be new, but the practice is old and the writer's feelings for his/her work are same in all the eras.

Quick recap of the history of writing in early days

We all know that in the early days writers used to carve stone with chisel and hammer to print their message or writings. It was impossible to erase or edit anything. Even before the invention of the words, writers used to convey their message through pictures. Many such scriptures have been dug out by archaeologists. A revolution came in the 11th century when Bi Sheng, a Chinese common man, invented the first movable ink type. The characters needed to be carved and the clay then needed to be fired. It wasn't very durable. Later, in the 12th century came wooden movable ink, the first of its kind. Jua Sui, another Chinese scholar, invented metal movable ink in the 14th century.

As Chinese were reaching milestones in ink inventions, Europe stepped in. In the 15th century, Gutenberg invented the first movable ink along with the printing press. Writers breathed a sigh of relief as the invention of the printing press became a very helpful medium for them. In 1780 the letter press machine was invented and turned the tables of writing and printing.

The first self-publisher, Ben Franklin, was followed by William Blake, and Virginia Woolf, who published their work in their own presses. William Blake designed the whole thing, wrote the texts of his best self-published work, which includes 'Songs of Experience', 'The Marriage of Heaven and Hell', and 'Songs of Innocence'. He engraved the manuscript on the copper plates, and then printed and coloured the pages to illustrate the manuscripts.

Self-publishing, as the word suggests is a privately printed written work with no involvement of any third party publisher. The writer/author holds the sole responsibility for the entire process of printing and publishing. The process becomes complex and multilevel in the case of books, as it includes the design of the cover, the format of the text, the price, marketing and distribution and public relations. There are agencies available, where these services can be outsourced by the author, who can hire them to do the entire book or parts of the process.

Jane Austen also tried her hand at self-publishing. Walt Whitman, an American poet, wrote, designed, and self-published the first edition of 'Leaves of Grass'. Marcel Proust's novel was rejected by a French publisher, but it didn't stop him from publishing 'Swann's Way'. It was the first edition of his seven volume masterpiece, 'Remembrance of Things Past'.

Publication houses have seen many ups and downs because of authors individually publishing their work. Authors felt that the publishers did not recognize their work enough. They were considering their literary work from a business point of view, which is right to some extent, but the works had more in them, which only the writers know. That is the reason the authors took the leash in their hands and made self-publishing the talk of the town. This is reflected by the Hogarth Press, which was started by Virgina Woolf and her husband, Leonard

Woolf. Virginia published her literary work and that of others in that press, which made it popular in those days. Its popularity can be measured by the several other presses started with the same idea. Dave Eggers and Kelly Link went the same route in writing and publishing as Virginia.

The question arises why more and more people are choosing self-publishing over traditional publishing houses. The following list of benefits will show why.

Speed up the process

It is obvious that time consumed with publication houses is way more than spent in self-publication. Self-published books are brought to the market in a few months or may be less. It's a speedy process. The internet has an important role in it. It has drastically decreased the time consumed at every step of the process. E-books are the latest additions to the book publishing sector. So, a writer doesn't have to wait for time-consuming formalities to launch his piece of work.

Control over everything

Authors/writers retain total control over the situation. You as a writer are the owner of the creative and technical process. Designing, formatting, distributing, price, etc.; nothing is beyond your reach. However, there is no such control in the case of Print on Demand Publishing (POD). You have to compromise at various levels, which most of us don't actually like to do when it comes to our own creative work.

All rights reserved

When a writer/author contacts publication houses s/he has to agree to many clauses inserted by the publisher. It sometimes destroys the retention of rights. The writer/author doesn't get the full royalty that s/he deserves. You may not like the cover page of your book, but because of the contract you signed you cannot do anything about it. It's an entirely different story with self-published books. All the rights belong to the author, giving him/her the freedom of doing whatever he/she wants with the book and its content at any time. Self-publishing lets you move out of the limited zone that POD publishers create for the artists.

Internet marketing

The publishing medium may have changed, but the rules are the same. Door-to-door marketing has become social media's profile-to-profile. Online stores have replaced the physical stores. Various free portals are available which you can use to market your hard cover, soft cover book, E-book and any kind of content. Even the paid portals don't charge you much, and they still give the deserving royalty and rights to the author. Promote it the way you wish to promote it.

Internet marketing or online marketing is an entirely different league. But if you know the ins and outs of it, then nothing can stop your book from getting in the list of most searched, read and even the best seller.

Avoid filling your shed

POD publishers allow sovereign writers to print their work as required rather than creating huge press runs, which leaves them with a stack of unsold books. Printing on order avoids this mess and allows you to save money otherwise spent on storing your large collection of the same book.

No time limit

Some publishers give a short deadline to the writer in which s/he has to complete the work. This destroys the creative process. The writer is worried about finishing the book on time rather than adding polish to the book by editing it in his/her own way.

No third party agent

The more people are involved, the less your cut of the deal. Agents may take a 15% to 20% share of every deal. The cut increases in some cases depending upon the requirement of the agent and brand value of the publication house.

Self-publishing may look easy at first glance. Well, it is easy if you know the 'HOW' of the things to do in the process. Thanks to the internet, you can gain enough knowledge about the 'How' to fully equip yourself with all the Dos and Don'ts in self-publishing. Here's a quick checklist for you before you decide to go for self-publishing.

First, let's check the Dos

Proof Read

Publication houses use high-salary paid editors to trim your content so that it reads better. You, on the other hand, may not have such skills, and so you have to do everything by yourself. Reading your content thoroughly will help you with that.

Learn about this business

You are a writer, a creative person, but you are not a genius salesman or marketing manager. You know how to present a story, but you do not know how to represent your book in the market. Learn a little bit of that before taking chances in the market. Simply put, you need to know the rules before you bend them.

Build your online presence

Get used to social media platforms. Establish yourself as a writer online. People should know about you as a writer, so that whenever you tell them to read what you have written, they read it seriously. Present yourself online as a brand.

Business cards

Carry a business card with you every time you go out. It should contain the contact and ordering information.

Reviews and Feedback

Get your work reviewed by your friends. These help in polishing your writing skills. If you are open enough then make visible your online reviews. There are readers in the market who choose a book based on the reviews.

Now, let's see some of the Don'ts

Don't target the bookstores

Self-publishing writers want readers, not bookstores. So, know your target audience. Approach the readers rather than selling to bookstores.

Don't pay unnecessary marketing costs

You can spend as much as you want when you start earning, but as a newbie in the field, make full use of free online advertising portals. There's a lot you can make out of them.

Stop annoying people

The most annoying thing fresh writers do is asking everyone every time they meet whether they have read their book. This destroys the credibility of the book every time you ask them this question. Ask them once, if they say no, change the topic. Don't be a pushy writer.

Don't expect high volume of sales at a signing

If we talk about Howard Stern or John Grisham, then book sales at signings go high, but an average author sells around 20 copies. So don't lose heart if your book signing doesn't fetch you a hefty amount of cash.

Don't destroy your relationships

A common mistake most new authors make is to insult the one who criticizes or rejects their work. You might write a book in the future which they like, and only they can publish. Don't destroy your personal or professional relationship with any professional in the industry.

Successful writers/authors are ready to learn the ins and outs of the business and publish the work on their own. The popularity of self-publishing clearly reflects the writers' choices. Book publishing has changed dramatically over the past couple of decades. Go, you are free to explore the world of self-publishing. Happy writing!

6) The Self-Publishing Process

So you've written your book, or perhaps you have a book concept that you think is unique. The only problem is, how do you get that idea and turn it into an actual volume on a bookshop shelf?

You enjoy the writing, you know your subject but you don't have the time or the inclination to learn the publishing business to ensure that you get the results that you want.

Writing

This is the bit we love to help you with! We interview the book out of you and take care of all the rest.

Editing and Critical Assessment

It takes skill and experience to read and critically assess a new manuscript, and it is a time consuming process.

In-depth editing also takes skill and time, and invariably an editor working closely with an author will improve a manuscript for publication. Editing can be time-consuming, and thus costly, and is best undertaken by an experienced literary editor.

Copy Editing

You've written the best book you can, checked your facts and double checked your spelling. Yet there will still be lots of mistakes! Particularly when you've lived with a project for a long time, you can become 'blind' to such mistakes, not spotting them until they're in print. The wrong caption, the wrong picture, inconsistent spelling, poor grammar, lack of punctuation... The copy editing process involves an independent party checking through your manuscript to look for such things and correct them. This ensures that your manuscript is of the highest quality (and you also get to approve any changes made before publication).

Formatting

First impressions count and you want your book to look good, inside and out. We will format your book to give that fantastic first impression. The formatting process involves taking a manuscript and converting it to how it will look in the book. We will use your text (from disk) and apply a typographical design to the book, placing photographs and graphics, choosing colours, page size, type size, etc. This will give the book a certain 'feel' and 'style' that will be carried through to the cover design. Once this process has been completed, you will be sent proofs to check (proof read).

Text and Cover Design

Take a look at any two books on your shelf and you'll notice how the appearance of their text is different. How do you decide what font to use, what weight, how large should the pages be (and what's the most economical size), what will make the page pleasing to the eye...?

Textual design is an art form which should not be overlooked. The best book can be ruined by poor typographical design, and if it's not easy to read, by and large people won't read it. We'll design your book and ensure that you're happy with that design before typesetting begins.

Cover design is arguably even more important, as it's often the cover that sells a book. How often have you seen 'home produced' books with terrible covers on the local bookshop shelf? We can design your book's jacket from scratch, using either your own artwork or supplying professional quality photographs or illustrations. We also ensure that your book cover includes a bar code - a necessity for stocking in bookshops.

ISBN Registration

There is no legal requirement to give your book an ISBN number. However, without an ISBN number, a book cannot be ordered through any bookshop (physical or online) as the book ordering systems all work using the unique ISBN number, not a book's title. The ISBN number is unique to every book, and it enables a book shop to identify the book's publisher, and thus be able to order it. Without an ISBN number on your book, you are effectively limiting yourself to private sales only.

Printing

The process of printing can be a minefield. Printing firms vary in equipment, the systems that they use and the price that they'll quote for the same job. How do you know exactly which quote will work out to be the best?

The printing industry has its own conventions and standards and if you don't know what these are you may not get the final product that you hoped for. There are also different printing processes - lithographic or digital? What are the differences? Which would be appropriate for your book? How do you tell a good printing company from a poor one? How many copies should be printed? What will reprints cost?

Authors should be aware of the differences between printing 'on demand' and printing copies in advance. With a print on demand (POD) book, no copies exist until someone buys one, at which point the book is printed and sent to the customer. POD books are thus almost exclusively sold through online retailers. The book trade works on a sale or return basis, so bookshops will rarely if ever pay to have copies of a POD book printed in the hope that they will then sell them.

POD is thus not only a form of printing, it is also a form of distribution. If you want to see your book on the shelves of a bookshop, then POD is not the correct form of distribution. You should opt instead to print a number of copies in advance (short run digital printing or litho printing) and have these distributed through the traditional book trade distribution channel of sale or return supply.

Bibliographic and Copyright Registration

How do booksellers know your book is available? They use various bibliographic databases run by companies such as Bowkers and Nielsen Book. These companies supply data to the high street and online bookstores, and you need to register with the databases so that your book appears on the stores' computer... invaluable when a customer wants to order it!

In addition, on publication you are required by law to send one copy of your book to the five Copyright Libraries in the UK, via the Copyright Receipt Office. We arrange registration for authors as a matter of course, and ensure the Deposit Libraries get their copies on your behalf.

Publicity and Marketing

Marketing and publicity are a part of publishing a book that many authors overlook; perhaps they are daunted by the prospect of 'selling' their book, or perhaps they simply don't know how. The books trade undoubtedly has complex distribution and sales systems which can appear to be impenetrable from the outside. Yet if you're serious about getting your book onto the shelves and selling more than a few copies, it's this part of the process that should demand your attention, even before the book has been printed.

Your book will also become available online via Amazon and other online retailers.

What nobody can do is guarantee sales of your book.

Distribution and Warehousing

Books that are distributed using the print on demand (POD) model exist only as entries on online retailers' websites until such time as a copy is bought by a reader. This avoids the need to print copies in advance, but it does effectively limit the sales of POD books to online retailers.

7) Why Did I Set Up Write My Expert Book?

After self-publishing my book on chiropractic, I was bitten by the writing bug and produced other books on aspects of health and running a small business, each of which at the time meant six months of hard slog.

I also began talking to chiropractic clients about their businesses and found that many of them, from all walks of life, were having to compete on price as I had done. They were having to sell themselves hard to all the potential clients and existing customers.

Many of the people I talked to would benefit from writing a book; for example, a builder who was doing large and very expensive projects. Because his clients didn't understand the complexity of the whole process, they were constantly whining, complaining, checking up on everything or changing things, and then getting upset when that added to the cost of the project.

Obviously people like the builder didn't have the time to write a book nor the inclination – perhaps they weren't very good at writing at school and didn't have the confidence to feel they could write.

The whole idea behind 'Write My Expert Book' is that instead of a person having to find the time to sit down and concentrate for a lengthy period of time on putting words to paper, 'Write My Expert Book' will interview the book out of them in very little time, take over all the other expert work that needs to be done, and at the end of the process, hand the author the keys to the book for him or her to use it to boost their business in the ways that we shall cover further on.

8) Why Would You Want To Publish Your Own Expert Book?

I wrote my first book purely because I am interested in the subject and I enjoy writing. The amazing effect that the book had on my business was a complete surprise to me. Since then I have come across many experts who have documented the benefits to your business of positioning yourself as an expert by writing your own expert book, including Dan Kennedy, Adam Witty, Steve Gordon and Daniel Priestley.

I highly recommend reading 'Key Person of Influence' by Daniel Priestley. He talks about how every industry revolves around key people of influence. I'm sure you know of such people in your industry. These people keep getting mentioned in conversation and they seem to earn more money and be more influential than everyone else, without appearing to work harder. In many cases it seems to be about who they know and their connections. Daniel's book is a great guide to getting to be the person that people want to know and work with. Daniel has shown in research across many industries that these "Key People" are in the top 5% of their industry but can earn many times what their colleagues earn.

Daniel recommends a five step process to becoming a 'Key Person of Influence' - I want to show you here how writing your own expert book fits into that process.

Have a clear and powerful pitch (also known as your "elevator speech"). You must quickly, clearly, and powerfully show that what you do has strong benefits to your audience. Getting your ideas into shape so that you can write a book about them forces you to express them in clear, concise and powerful. I have also found that in interviewing my clients as part of the Write My Expert Book process we are going through a coaching process which draws out the unique features and benefits of their work.

Publish – gain credibility by authoring content. If you have written 'the book' you must be an expert! Later I will show you how to re-purpose the content of your book so you can leverage your expertise in lots of different formats.

Productise your information. Horrible phrase, but what he means is organise all the knowledge you have in your industry so that it becomes something people want to buy. This could mean added value to your customers so they want to pay you more for your service than they will pay your competitors. It can also mean becoming the guru in your industry so that you get paid for consultancy and coaching. What is the best way to organise your knowledge into a product? Write a book.

Profile – how to become known, liked and trusted in your industry. You will need to write your book to the right target audience. If you intend to become a coach to your colleagues you will aim the book at them. If you intend to sell more of your products and services to your customers you aim the book at them.

Partnership – the ability to build and maintain strategic relationships. In my case I have found that other professionals are happier to work with me and refer to me because I have 'written the book'. If you were an orthodontist you would find that referring dentists want to be associated with you because your expert status rubs off on them. In every industry people want to find partners they can trust to get the work done reliably. How better to quickly demonstrate that you know everything you need to know to get the job done than to write your own book, especially if it is crammed with stories about your happy customers.

In Steve Gordon's book 'Unstoppable Referrals' Steve talks about using a 'referral kit'. The referral kit is a package of information that you give to a client or referral partner. This information is designed to affect the potential client in four ways:

1. It helps them understand the problem and the consequences of doing nothing

2. It helps them make sense of the possible solutions

3. It suggests a first step to solve the problem, for example a meeting with you

4. It elevates your expert status in the potential client's mind and builds trust

Steve outlines the five advantages of using the referral kit:

1. No sales pressure. Your clients and referral partners aren't hesitant to give out a book when they could be wary of a direct introduction because of putting friends into a 'sales pitch'.

2. It's a gift with no strings attached and builds the status of the referrer. (How many people know someone who has written a book?)

3. It positions you above the scrum of competitors and you can spell out your Unique Selling Proposition.

4. It is easy to pass along and acts as your 'business in a box'.

5. It adds value. If done correctly you have given potential customers a lot of information. Often our clients are

worried about giving away too much information. Don't worry about that – if the reader is considering doing a DIY job they are not the right client for you. For example if I wanted help with writing a will, the lawyer would spell out all the pitfalls and things to look out for, and I would ask them to do the work because I understood the consequences of getting it wrong.

Steve goes through various formats for the referral kit but is very much in favour of the book because of the status our society gives to printed books, and because writing a book is perceived as a difficult thing to do.

The biggest problem I have found is that there are many people with a huge wealth of experience who don't realise that, not only could they write their own expert book, but that there would be many benefits to their business in doing so. I was talking to someone recently who had 35 years in the double-glazing industry and knew absolutely everything there was to know about how to get the best results from installing double-glazing, which company to go for, what to look out for, how to avoid scams, etc. etc. But as there is only him and a colleague running the business, there's absolutely no time for him to sit down and actually write the book, nor would he have the first idea how to start.

9) How Would That Impact On Your Business?

Whatever industry you're in, you have to compete with everyone else on price because there are no other criteria that people can judge you on. Unless you've had a fantastic referral from a satisfied client you simply can't spread the word about your skills and expertise quickly enough. If you're trying to break into a new niche market, you might have a lot of experience in a similar niche but you don't have any referrals or contacts in the new niche. Because there is so much competition you get a lot time wasters; if you're in the building trade for example, you will be asked for an awful lot of quotations, very few of which will even get a response from a potential customer.

10) Who Would Benefit From Writing Their Own Expert Book'?

Specific examples of the people who might benefit, ones that leap to mind from my background are coaches, masseurs, chiropractors, osteopaths, physiotherapists, medical practitioners, who are working privately or in a specific niche, and dentists. For example, there are two options for dentists: if you're an orthodontist that other dentists refer to, you can write your book aimed at the other dentists, or you could write a book aimed at the general public on how to improve your smile.

Anyone involved in high-value projects might benefit, so if you install swimming pools, build extensions or houses, or if you are an architect, your customers have to be pretty certain that you're the right person to handle the job. Certainly, from my point of view, if there was a well-written book from an architect I'd be far more likely to go to them than to anyone else. They can demonstrate all their expertise in one place and if I'm involved in paying out a lot of money for a project, I need a lot of reassurance that I'm picking the right person and I can put my trust in that person.

Another group of people that could benefit from writing an expert book would be people that are employed in a company, so for example, if you are a solicitor working for a big firm of solicitors and your specialist role within the company is tax law, for example, then if you write an expert book on current tax law, your value to that company has increased exponentially. So that company can use that book to bring in business and the likelihood of being promoted and pay rises etc. will therefore increase.

11) What Could You Call Your 'Expert Book'?

Here are some ideas for different industries. As part of the process of coaching your book out of you we will bring out the key benefits to your customers and these key benefits go into the title of your book.

A catchy, 'selling' book title in some cases emerges spontaneously from the mind of the author, the editor or from someone in the publisher's marketing or sales department. More commonly, however, writing a book title-- like everything else about attentively publishing a book-- involves work.

Step 1: Determine exactly what concepts you want your book title to get across

Keeping in mind the book's promise to readers, make a list of ideas of what you would like the title to communicate, and the psychological response you would like target readers to have, and words that suggest those ideas.

Step 2: Brainstorm book title concepts

Generate a lot of book title ideas around the contents of the book - words, phrases, fragments. Make your list as long as possible. Don't worry if the concepts are silly or odd-- do not restrict yourself or evaluate your list at this point, just get them down on paper (maybe even on index cards).

To assist you brainstorm your book title, you can make use of the aid of an online book title generator along with this fun method, which imitates exactly what frequently happens in some book publisher's product packaging meetings. Gather some friends of friends to help (more neutral than actual friends; bribing them with food and drink typically works). Share with the group the list of ideas and emotional responses you made in step 1 and tell them to go at it. Bear in mind, no judgments! In her memoir, 'My Life in France', Julia Child composed that a few of the 'brainstormed' early ideas included: French Magicians in the Kitchen, Method in Cuisine Madness, French Cooking from the American Supermarket, The Witchcraft of French Cooking, and Food-France-Fun.

If your book needs a subtitle, make use of the same technique for conceptualising subtitles to complement your title.

For a non-fiction book title, writing a great title typically includes crafting a concrete guarantee, a clear advantage statement regarding what the reader can expect to learn about. Some good, straightforward examples include: 'The 4-Hour Workweek' (Tim Ferriss's first title for his bestselling 'The 4-Hour Workweek' was 'How to Buy Drugs Legally Online'!)

Non-fiction books usually also get subtitles.

Step 3: Refine your book title

Some book title concepts will certainly seem naturally much better than others; curtail your list of titles (together with appropriate subtitles, if appropriate).

Step 4: Research your book's competition

After your brainstorming and narrowing, you should Google your book title and look it up on Amazon.com. Occasionally your most dazzling concept is ... already out there. And, while you cannot copyright a title you ought to understand (and beware) of marketplace confusion.

Is the coast clear for your top book title picks?

Step 5: Socialise and ask for viewpoints

Mingle your leading options for a book title: get the opinions of others who you trust - readers in your category in addition to your local booksellers and librarians are good choices. In spite of all your own book title work, showing the leading contenders around might simply stimulate an idea you had not yet thought about, for example:

- How to choose a builder who can get your extension built on time, on budget and to the highest standard.

- Spas: Planning, Selecting and Installing (Ortho Books)

- Will Writing For the Single Daddy: How to Write a Will for the Single Dad

- Architect and Client: Choosing an Architect

- Choosing Your Builder: Choosing Your Builder (Building a House Advice Book 4)

- How to Choose A Swimming Pool Contractor: 4 (Swimming Pool Ownership and Care)

- Choosing a Dance School: 8 Essential Questions Every Parent Should Ask

12) How to Use Your Expert Book

One of the easiest ways to drive prospective clients and customers to your business is to become the expert in your field. The term "expert" carries credibility and prestige that can open many doors for you, and, oddly enough, the term is relatively easy to acquire. This simple three step process can help you quickly and easily set yourself up as the expert in your field.

Step 1: Determine Your Niche

Instead of trying to be everything to everybody, narrow down your focus to the things that you are really, really good at. A friend of mine set himself up as an expert at leadership training for water treatment facilities. When he told me what he was doing, I asked, "Is there any money in that?" He smiled and said, "Every city's got one, and I'm the only leadership expert in this field in the country." He was frequently quoted in trade journals and asked to speak at their conventions. Find your niche, and you'll eliminate your competition.

Step 2: Write about Your Area of Expertise

After you determine your niche, begin to write articles about your area of expertise. Every single day, tens of thousands of editors, webmasters and newsletter publishers are looking doggedly for unique and information-packed articles. If you can write articles that teach readers about your industry, you will find numerous places that will quickly publish your article.

Write a few articles, and you can become a recognized expert in any field.

Step 3: Speak as Often as You Can

When your articles begin to get published, you'll start to receive requests to speak more often.

95% of the population has some type of nervousness about public speaking. So when you stand up and say what you want to say, the way you want to say it, you are doing what 95% of the population wish they could do. When you speak about your industry, you set yourself up as the expert on that topic. You gain instant credibility.

If you get nervous when you speak in front of a group, attend a public speaking class. It will be the best investment of your life, because the more confident you present your ideas, the more competent you will appear in front of a group.

Follow these three simple steps and you will become the recognised expert in your specific niche.

The first thing to do is to actually get the book written and 'Write My Expert Book' makes that very easy for you. There are many ways you can use the book to promote your expert status and to promote sales:

Hand out the book to your customers - **this will improve** compliance and stop lots of questions being asked, because you've answered them in the book. There will be less price resistance because your customer has already decided that you're the one.

It also makes it much easier for people to refer, for example, they might say 'you must go to Joe Blogs because he's not just any old builder, he's written the book on building', or 'you should go to Fred, he's the best life coach and he really understands people because he's written a book about this specific issue'.

Give the book out to previous customers - it boosts re-activation and will also help with referrals.

Cross-sell - your company might offer a range of services but the customer who has bought one service from you may not realise that you offer other related services that they could buy from you. Cross-selling improves the lifetime value of each customer, and makes them a long-term customer. Unlike an e-book, (90% of which never get read and take up space on your hard drive), the advantage with a paper book is that it's sitting on your shelf. It's staring at you every time you look at the shelf, and you're constantly reminded of it. It's easy to refer to. You can put a bookmark in one place and show it to your friend very easily.

Use it at networking events – you can make a 30 second conversation with someone very specific, for example by saying my name is XYZ and I'm an expert in ABC. How can I help you? Build on that conversation with "I've got far too much information to give you in our limited time, would you like me to send you a copy of my book?" Once you've got their name and address, you can follow up by direct mail which is far more powerful than an email.

Include the book in the marketing funnel as a purchase – once you've got the contact's details, move them further down the marketing funnel and turn them into a proper prospect by getting them to make a small purchase, such as your book, for just the cost of production and postage.

They've had to pay you a small amount, so they've turned into a customer. Follow with direct mail. A letter feels more important because nowadays they are so few and far between. If it's properly delivered it comes across as a very personal communication.

Use the audio – once the initial interview has been done, the audio can be edited and tidied and can be used as a webinar, again establishing you as an expert.

Do a podcast – you can be interviewed about your book. Write My Expert Book can arrange for a podcast to be produced.

Go on local radio – send an edited section of the audio and a hard copy of the book to the local radio producers. You're demonstrating that: (a) you're an expert because you've written a book and (b) you come over well in interviews. You've taken all the risk out of the selection process for the radio producers. They know that you will come over well on their program and that you are able to talk about interesting things. There are many things you can do once you've got into local radio but it's all about boosting your expert status, and it's free publicity. You're going to be heard by 30,000 at absolutely no cost to you.

Use a Virtual Assistant – now you've got the audio which has been transcribed, sections of the transcription can be turned into expert articles to be put on blogs, used as an e-course, or as a free initial offering in your marketing funnel.

Comment on industry specific forums – your status in the forum would be as a published author, not as someone selling their services, because you don't need to – you're the expert. Your message is simply to help, and you can send them a free copy of your book if they let you have their contact details.
The aim is to change the relationship between you and your prospects from being a pest trying to sell something to being the expert offering to give lots of free help and advice. By establishing trust, you become the first person they call when they need a particular job doing.

Get a voice over artist to record your book as an audio book – This is especially valuable if your customers are on the road a lot of the time. For example quantity surveyors, builders, sales reps, doctors or therapists making house calls, managers traveling for meetings. There are services like Createspace and Kunaki.com which can produce small quantities of CDs with high quality packaging at very low cost. They can even handle orders, shipping and returns directly with your customer.

Use the book as the basis for your expert presentations – Introduce yourself to potential speaking engagements as the published author of an expert book. They will immediately know that you know what you are talking about, you will be introduced to your audience as the expert published author, and the presentation becomes a valuable lesson from an industry leader rather than just another sales pitch. During your talk you give good information with no sales pitch. At the end you say "If you want to know more I have some copies of my book to give away – I don't have enough for everyone but if you give me your name and address I will post you a copy at my expense" No sales pressure but you are collecting highly qualified leads.

13) Why Become The Expert?

The end result of establishing yourself as an expert is that you would be unique in your industry so there would be no other builder around, for example, who has written a book on how to build the best kitchen extension at the best cost or whatever; and because you're different and you're the expert, you're no longer competing on price. You're no longer just one of a commodity service where people can shop around. If you are the only expert, there is no-one else to shop with.

14) How Is Our Approach Different and Better Than Anyone Else In the Self-Publishing Industry?

The way 'My Expert Book' has been set up is that it is very specific and very targeted at boosting the profit of your business. This is not about vanity publishing. Your book needs to have a specific purpose and that purpose is to be a very long form sales letter. The format of the book is a classical letter format: you introduce yourself, identify the problem, agitate the problem, and then solve the problem. You lead customers through this process at the end of which the only possible resource for a resolution of their problem is your product or service.

These books are not aimed at people who want to be on the best seller lists. There are other companies who will get you on to the New York Times best seller list involving a lot more work and a lot more expense. These books are designed to be small, easily read, in a conversational style that people find very approachable and palatable, and very specific to establishing your credibility as the go-to expert in your field. The major benefit is they take much less time than sitting down and trying to write a whole book yourself. The whole process is much easier.

15) How Do We Help You Become The Expert?

The book that you are reading at the moment was written using our book-writing process. It is a good example of how you can use the book. There is a list of resources at the end to help you publicise the book and use it the right way. The other benefit of the 'Write My Expert Book' process is that in preparing yourself by going through the starting questionnaire, you clarify your thoughts so that you can be interviewed about your expert industry. This forces you to refine your own ideas about your business. In effect you're also getting coaching about your business, as well as writing the book. If you're clear enough about your business that you can write a book about it, and communicate your business to your readers, you're also prepared to talk to an audience; from a stage, on the radio, on television, and at networking groups.

16) How can 'Write My Expert Book' help?

Our initial consultation will enable us to determine whether you need to write a book, and whether it would be a suitable process for you. Once we have established the 'My Expert Book' is for you, we will send you a list of interview questions to help you prepare for interview. You would be interviewed. Once the interview has been transcribed, Write My Expert Book will do all the proof reading, editing, fact checking, formatting and cover design. We can also help with getting a suitable title that would be impressive and sell-able. We'll get the cover design done and formatted, and set up the self-publishing account. At the end of the process, we hand you the keys to your self-publishing empire and you take it from there.

17) Your Next Step

Contact us to arrange a 30 minute conversation to see whether self-publishing would actually help your business. We need to determine whether you have enough information or expertise to put into a book and whether your business is established in a way that a book would be helpful.

18) The future for 'Write My Expert Book'

I plan to grow the self-publishing business. I am constantly looking for new ways to help people in the self-publishing industry, so, as well as doing the whole process from start to finish we can also help with individual sections. Some people prefer to sit down and write the bulk of the copy themselves, but we can then take over and do the editing, proof reading, formatting and cover design and so on, or we can take individual sections of the work and do that. We can also advise on whether the copy produced so far is the right format to sell your services. It may be that you've written a very good book, but it doesn't lead the reader through to purchasing your services. We can also help with whom you aim your book at, for example, business to business, which would have a certain language style, or business to consumers which would have a different language style.

19) Acknowledgments

I would like to thank my lovely wife Janet for the years and years of putting up with me working too hard and writing too many e-books, and looking after the seven children while she's doing all that, and also trying to set up her perfume business and writing her own novel. And I would also like to thank my colleagues at Penrith Family Chiropractic for helping me find the time to establish this business and also to Dan Kennedy and Nigel Botterill for all their advice and training.

20) References

No B.S. Marketing to the Affluent: The No Holds Barred, Kick Butt, Take No Prisoners Guide to Getting Really Rich (Jul 2008) - Dan Kennedy

Book the Business: How to Make Big Money with Your Book Without Even Selling a Single Copy Paperback (Oct 2013) - Adam Witty and Dan Kennedy

Botty's Rules: 29 Success Secrets From the UK Entrepreneur Who's Been There and Done it…(Aug 2011) – Nigel Botterill

Key Person of Influence (Revised Edition): The Five-Step Method to Become One of the Most Highly Valued and Highly Paid People in Your Industry (Sept 2014)

Unstoppable Referrals – Steve Gordon

21) Resources

Book interviews and pod casts – Viv Oyalu www.audio-byte.co.uk

For general business advice – Entrepreneurs Circle
www.entrepreneurscircle.org

22) Contact details

Peter Bennett – peter@writemyexpertbook.com

23) Special offer

Would your business benefit from an Expert Book?

To claim a free, no obligation phone consultation with Peter to see if your business could benefit from your own expert book just email Peter on info@writemyexpertbook.com

www.ingramcontent.com/pod-product-compliance
Lightning Source LLC
Chambersburg PA
CBHW072302170526
45158CB00003BA/1150